THE 30-MINUTE SHAKESPEARE

# THE MERRY WIVES OF WINDSOR

"Nick Newlin's work as a teaching artist for Folger Education during the past thirteen years has provided students, regardless of their experience with Shakespeare or being on stage, a unique opportunity to tread the boards at the Folger Theatre. Working with students to edit Shakespeare's plays for performance at the annual Folger Shakespeare Festivals has enabled students to gain new insights into the Bard's plays, build their skills of comprehension and critical reading, and just plain have fun working collaboratively with their peers.

Folger Education promotes performance-based teaching of Shakespeare's plays, providing students with an interactive approach to Shakespeare's plays in which they participate in a close reading of the text through intellectual, physical, and vocal engagement. Newlin's *The 30-Minute Shakespeare* series is an invaluable resource for teachers of Shakespeare, and for all who are interested in performing the plays."

**ROBERT YOUNG, PH.D.**
DIRECTOR OF EDUCATION
FOLGER SHAKESPEARE LIBRARY

The Merry Wives of Windsor: The 30-Minute Shakespeare
ISBN 978-1-935550-05-1
Adaptation, essays, and notes © 2010 by Nick Newlin

Cover design by Sarah Juckniess
Printed in the United States of America

Distributed by Consortium Book Sales & Distribution
www.cbsd.com


NICOLO WHIMSEY PRESS
www.30MinuteShakespeare.com

Art Director: Sarah Juckniess
Managing Editor: Katherine Little

A PLEASANT CONCEITED COMEDIE
of SIR JOHN FALSTAFF and

# THE MERRY WIVES
# OF WINDSOR

THE 30-MINUTE SHAKESPEARE

Written by WILLIAM SHAKESPEARE

Abridged AND Edited
by NICK NEWLIN

Nicolo Whimsey
Press

Brandywine, MD

*To Joanne*
*My muse*
*My merry wife*

Special thanks to Joanne Flynn, Bill Newlin, Eliza Newlin Carney, William and Louisa Newlin, Michael Tolaydo, Hilary Kacser, Sarah Juckniess, Katherine Little, Eva Zimmerman, Julie Schaper and all of Consortium, Leo Bowman and the students, faculty, and staff at Banneker Academic High School, and Robert Young Ph.D., and the Folger Shakespeare Library, especially the wonderful Education Department.

# ✳ TABLE OF CONTENTS

# ✳ NO EXPERIENCE NECESSARY

I was not a big "actor type" in high school, so if you weren't either, or if the young people you work with are not, then this book is for you. Whether or not you work with "actor types," you can use this book to stage a lively and captivating thirty-minute version of a Shakespeare play. No experience is necessary.

When I was about eleven years old, my parents took me to see Shakespeare's *Two Gentlemen of Verona*, which was being performed as a Broadway musical. I didn't comprehend every word I heard, but I was enthralled with the language, the characters, and the story, and I understood enough of it to follow along. From then on, I associated Shakespeare with *fun*.

Of course Shakespeare is fun. The Elizabethan audiences knew it, which is one reason he was so popular. It didn't matter that some of the language eluded them. The characters were passionate and vibrant, and their conflicts were compelling. Young people study Shakespeare in high school, but more often than not they read his work like a text book and then get quizzed on academic elements of the play, such as plot, theme, and vocabulary. These are all very interesting, but not nearly as interesting as standing up and performing a scene! It is through performance that the play comes alive and all its "academic" elements are revealed. There is nothing more satisfying to a student or teacher than the feeling of "owning" a Shakespeare play, and that can only come from performing it.

But Shakespeare's plays are often two or more hours long, making the performance of an entire play almost out of the question. One can perform a single scene, which is certainly a good start, but what about the story? What about the changes a character goes through as the play progresses? When school groups perform one scene unedited, or when they lump several plays together, the audience can get lost. This is why I have always preferred to tell the story of the play.

*The 30-Minute Shakespeare* gives students and teachers a chance to get up on their feet and act out a Shakespeare play in half an hour, using his language. The emphasis is on key scenes, with narrative bridges between scenes to keep the audience caught up on the action. The stage directions are built into this script so that young actors do not have to stand in one place; they can move and tell the story with their actions as well as their words. And it can all be done in a classroom during class time!

That is where this book was born: not in a research library, a graduate school lecture, a professional stage, or even an after-school drama club. All of the play cuttings in *The 30-Minute Shakespeare* were first rehearsed in a D.C. public high school English class, and performed successfully at the Folger Shakespeare Library's annual Secondary School Shakespeare Festival. The players were not necessarily "actor types." For many of them, this was their first performance in a play.

Something almost miraculous happens when students perform Shakespeare. They "get" it. By occupying the characters and speaking the words out loud, students gain a level of understanding and appreciation that is unachievable by simply reading the text. That is the magic of a performance-based method of learning Shakespeare, and this book makes the formerly daunting task of staging a Shakespeare play possible for anybody.

With *The 30-Minute Shakespeare* book series I hope to help teachers and students produce a Shakespeare play in a short amount of time, thus jump-starting the process of discovering the beauty, magic, and fun of the Bard. Plot, theme, and language reveal themselves through the performance of these half-hour play cuttings, and everybody involved receives the priceless gift of "owning" a piece of Shakespeare. The result is an experience that is fun and engaging, and one that we can all carry with us as we play out our own lives on the stages of the world.

**NICK NEWLIN**
*Brandywine, MD*
*March 2010*

# CHARACTERS IN THE PLAY

*The following is a list of characters that appear in this cutting of*
The Merry Wives of Windsor.

*Twenty actors performed in the original production. This number
can be increased to about thirty or decreased to about twelve by having
actors share or double roles.*

*For the full breakdown of characters, see Sample Program.*

**SIR JOHN FALSTAFF:** A knight

**MISTRESS ALICE FORD**

**MISTRESS MARGARET PAGE**

**PISTOL**

**NYM** } Followers of Falstaff

**BARDOLPH**

**HOST OF THE GARTER INN**

**MASTER FRANCIS FORD**

**MASTER GEORGE PAGE** } Gentlemen of Windsor

**DR. CAIUS:** A French physician

**SIR HUGH EVANS:** A Welsh parson

**MISTRESS QUICKLY:** Servant to Dr. Caius

**ROBIN:** Page to Falstaff

**SERVANTS**

**NARRATORS**

# ✳ **SCENE 1.** (ACT I, SCENE III)

*The tavern at the Garter Inn.*

STAGEHANDS *place table and five stools center stage, slightly downstage of the pillars. The table is covered with a tablecloth and set with a candleholder and candle, three mugs, a wine bottle, and silverware.*

*Enter* NARRATOR *from stage rear, coming downstage.*

*As* NARRATOR *introduces the roles, players enter from stage rear, cross the stage in character, and exit stage right (see Performance Notes).*

**NARRATOR**
> We open at the Garter Inn, run by its gregarious host. The fat knight, Sir John Falstaff, is accompanied by Pistol, Nym, Bardolph, and Robin, his band of rogues and thieves. Falstaff hatches a plot to woo Mistress Page and Mistress Ford simultaneously.

*Exit* NARRATOR *stage left.*

*Enter* HOST *from stage rear, whistling to himself and carrying a mug and a rag.*

*Enter* FALSTAFF, PISTOL, NYM, ROBIN, *and* BARDOLPH. FALSTAFF *is in the lead, swaggering and chortling.* PISTOL *and* NYM *are jostling for position, followed by* ROBIN, *who has thick glasses and bad eyesight. Last comes* BARDOLPH, *attempting to juggle and drink from a flask simultaneously.* FALSTAFF *corralls them all to the table and sits on the center stool, flanked closely by* PISTOL *on his right and* NYM *on his left.*

**FALSTAFF** *(bangs a mug on the table)*
Mine host of the garter!

**HOST**
What says my bullyrook? Speak scholarly and wisely.

HOST *pours* FALSTAFF *a drink, denying* PISTOL'S *and* NYM'S *desire for drinks as well. When the two attempt to sip from* FALSTAFF'S, *he swats them away.*

**FALSTAFF**
Truly, mine host, I must turn away some of my followers.

**HOST**
Discard, bully Hercules: cashier. Let them wag: trot, trot!

HOST *makes a horse trotting motion and starts trotting around the room.* BARDOLPH *joins in for the fun of it.*

**FALSTAFF** *(looks despondently in his purse)*
I sit at ten pounds a week.

**HOST** *(bows down to him)*
Thou'rt an emperor, Caesar, Keisar, and Pheezar.
*(looks over at* BARDOLPH, *who is busy trying to extract the last drops from the bottle of wine.)* I will entertain Bardolph: he shall draw, he shall tap.

**HOST**
I have spoke: let him follow. *(to* BARDOLPH) Let me see thee froth and lime. I am at a word: follow.

**FALSTAFF**
> Bardolph, follow him. A tapster is a good trade.
> Go; adieu.

**BARDOLPH** *draws himself up, proudly. In fact, this is the proudest moment of his life. He gets up on the table . . .*

**BARDOLPH**
> It is a life that I have desired: I will thrive!

*. . . pulls out his juggling balls and juggles! The others are amazed, and applaud and laugh.*

**HOST** *whistles and gestures to* **BARDOLPH** *to follow him.* **BARDOLPH** *descends from the table in a grandiose fashion, pretending the bottle is a beer tap. He notices there is still a drop left so he shakes it onto his hand and licks his hand with delight.*

**PISTOL**
> O base Hungarian wight! Wilt thou the spigot wield?

**NYM**
> He was gotten in drink: is not the humor conceited?
> *(laughs a funny laugh)*

**FALSTAFF**
> I am glad I am so acquit of this tinderbox. His
> thefts were too open. *(checks his purse again and
> sighs; examines his shoe)* I am almost out at heels.

**PISTOL**
> Why, then, let kibes ensue. *(PISTOL and NYM laugh
> hysterically)*

**FALSTAFF** *(laughs and elbows PISTOL, then tries to think)*
> There is no remedy: I must cony-catch, I must Shift.

PISTOL *draws closer, conspiring and rubbing his hands.* NYM *draws closer as well, wanting to be in on the action.*

**PISTOL**

>Young ravens must have food. *(notices the fork and pockets it)*

**FALSTAFF**

>Which of you know Ford of this town?

**PISTOL**

>I ken the wight: he is of substance good.

**FALSTAFF**

>My honest lads, I will tell you what I am about.

**PISTOL**

>Two yards and more.

PISTOL *and* NYM *laugh.* NYM *continues until he looks around and realizes he is the only one laughing. He stops abruptly.*

**FALSTAFF**

>No quips now, Pistol! Indeed, I am in the waist
>two yards about; but I am now about no waste: I
>am about thrift. Briefly, I do mean to make love to
>Ford's wife. *(*PISTOL *and* NYM *are more than amused,
>but they are also curious)* I spy entertainment in her:
>*(starts to sashay around the room, imitating a lady)*
>she discourses, she carves, she gives the leer
>of invitation.

**NYM**

>The anchor is deep: Will that humor pass?

**FALSTAFF**

> Now, the report goes she has all the rule of her
> husband's purse: he hath a legion of angels. (*looks*
> *heavenward in anticipation of riches*)

**PISTOL**

> As many devils entertain; (*leaping to his feet*) and
> "To her, boy," say I.

**NYM** (*leaping to his feet*)

> The humor rises; it is good. Humor me the angels.

**FALSTAFF** (*pulls out the letters with a flourish, proudly revealing*
> *the plan*)
> I have writ me here a letter to her: and here another
> to Page's wife, who even now gave me good eyes too,
> examined my parts with most judicious oeillades.
> Sometimes the beam of her view gilded my foot,
> sometimes my portly belly.

**PISTOL**

> Then did the sun on dunghill shine.

**NYM**

> I thank thee for that humor.

**FALSTAFF**

> Here's another letter to her: she bears the purse
> too. She is a region in Guiana, all gold and bounty.
> I will be cheaters to them both, and they shall be
> exchequers to me, (*draws the men to either side*
> *of him, arms around them*) They shall be my East
> and West Indies and I will trade to them both.
> (*to* **NYM**) Go bear thou this letter to Mistress Page;
> (*to* **PISTOL**) and thou this to Mistress Ford. We will

thrive, lads, we will thrive! *(tries to hand them the letters, but they both turn away)*

**PISTOL** *(draws away indignantly)*
Shall I Sir Pandarus of Troy become
And by my side wear steel? Then, Lucifer take all!
*(hands the letter back gruffly)*

**NYM**
I will run no base humor. Here, take the humor-letter: I will keep the havior of reputation. *(hands the letter back)*

**FALSTAFF** *(slightly confused by this turn of events, then angry; he wants the letters delivered, so he turns to* **ROBIN**)
Hold, sirrah, bear you these letters tightly.
Sail like my pinnace to these golden shores! *(hands him the letters)*
*(turns angrily toward* **PISTOL** *and* **NYM**; *rises and draws himself up powerfully)* Rogues, hence, avaunt! vanish like hailstones, go!
Trudge, plod away o' the hoof; seek shelter, pack
Falstaff will learn the humor of the age,
French thrift, you rogues: myself and skirted page.

*Exit* **FALSTAFF** *and* **ROBIN** *stage right.* **ROBIN** *is squinting, trying desperately to read the letters, wiping his glasses clean. He bumps into the wall on his way out.*

**PISTOL**
Let vultures gripe thy guts! Base Phrygian Turk!

**NYM**
I have operations which be humors of revenge.

**PISTOL**

Wilt thou revenge?

**NYM**

With both the humors, I. I will discuss the humor of
this love to Page.

**PISTOL**

And I to Ford shall eke unfold
how Falstaff, varlet vile,
his dove will prove, his gold will hold,
and his soft couch defile.

**NYM**

My humor shall not cool. I will incense Page to deal
with poison. I will possess him with yellowness, for
the revolt of mine is dangerous: that is my true humor.

**PISTOL**

Thou art the Mars of malcontents.
I second thee: troop on!

PISTOL *and* NYM *clear the table of whatever goods are left.* PISTOL
*stuffs the candleholder in his pocket;* NYM *is about to leave, then
as an afterthought takes the tablecloth and stuffs it into his shirt.*

*Exit* PISTOL *and* NYM *stage right, stomping off arm in arm.*

# ✳ SCENE 2. (ACT III, SCENE III)

*A laundry room in the Ford household.*

**STAGEHANDS** *remove stools and props and place chairs around table, setting it with a tablecloth, two teacups, a vase, and a mirror.*

*Enter* **NARRATOR** *from stage rear, coming downstage.*

*As* **NARRATOR** *introduces the roles, players enter from stage rear, cross the stage in character, and exit stage right (see Performance Notes).*

**NARRATOR**
> Mistress Ford and Mistress Page are having some fun leading Falstaff on. This throws Master Ford into a jealous rage. Accompanied by his friend Master Page and those manglers of the English language, the Welsh parson Sir Hugh Evans and the French Doctor Caius, he attempts to discover Falstaff in the process of wooing these women.

*Exit* **NARRATOR** *stage rear.*

*Enter* **MISTRESS FORD** *and* **MISTRESS PAGE** *from stage right.* **MISTRESS PAGE** *carries with her a purse containing a comb and makeup so she can "freshen up" at any time.* **MISTRESS FORD** *is generally more relaxed in her physical demeanor.*

**MISTRESS FORD** *(looks under the table for the basket, which is not there; she is a little frustrated and*

*somewhat panicked)*
What, John! What, Robert!

**MISTRESS PAGE** *(also in somewhat of a panic)*
Quickly, quickly! Is the buck-basket—

*Enter* **SERVANTS** *(John and Robert) from stage right, carrying a basket of laundry. They engage in a tug of war with the basket, which escalates into a clothing fight using the dirty laundry.*

**MISTRESS FORD**
I warrant. What, Robert, I say!
Here, set it down. John and Robert, be ready here hard by in the brew-house: and when I suddenly call you, come forth, and without any pause or staggering take this basket on your shoulders: that done, trudge with it in all haste, and carry it among the whitsters in Datchet-mead, and there empty it in the muddy ditch close by the Thames side.

**MISTRESS PAGE**
You will do it? *(***SERVANTS*** nod)*

*Exit* **SERVANTS** *stage left, leaving the basket and continuing their laundry fight.*

**MISTRESS FORD** *and* **MISTRESS PAGE** *sit, the former fluffing her hair and straightening her dress and the latter fixing her makeup.*

**MISTRESS PAGE**
Here comes little Robin.

*Enter* **ROBIN** *from stage left, still fumbling and cleaning his glasses. His first comments are directed not to* **MISTRESS FORD** *but to the pillar.*

**ROBIN** *(to pillar)*
 Mistress Ford!

**MISTRESS FORD** *is amused, goes to* **ROBIN**, *and leads him by the hand to where she is sitting.*

**ROBIN**
 My master, Sir John, is come in at your back-door, Mistress Ford, and requests your company.

**MISTRESS PAGE**
 I'll go hide me.

**MISTRESS PAGE** *hides behind stage rear curtain, and peeks out occasionally during the action that follows.*

**MISTRESS FORD** *(to* **ROBIN***)*
 Go tell thy master I am alone.

*Exit* **ROBIN** *stage left.*

**MISTRESS FORD**
 Mistress Page, remember you your cue.

**MISTRESS PAGE** *(poking her head out from behind curtain)*
 I warrant thee; if I do not act it, hiss me.
  *(demonstrates with a hissing sound)*

**MISTRESS FORD**
 Go to, then: we'll use this unwholesome humidity, this gross watery pumpion; we'll teach him to know turtles from jays. *(sits in chair stage left of table and continues to fuss with her hair and dress)*

*Enter* **FALSTAFF** *from stage left, swaggering lasciviously.*

MISTRESS FORD *stifles a laugh at* FALSTAFF, *who bends down on one knee in front of the chair, kissing her hand and then her arm. She pulls away, and he practically flops into the basket.*

**FALSTAFF**
> Have I caught thee, my heavenly jewel? Why, now let me die, for I have lived long enough: this is the period of my ambition: O this blessed hour!

MISTRESS FORD *stands and casts a glance at the curtain behind her.* MISTRESS PAGE *sticks her head out and they both giggle.*

**MISTRESS FORD**
> O sweet Sir John!

MISTRESS FORD *tousles his hair and he shivers with delight.* MISTRESS PAGE *moves to the stage right chair and* FALSTAFF *follows, shuffling on his knees.*

**FALSTAFF**
> Mistress Ford, I cannot cog, I cannot prate, I would make thee my lady.

**MISTRESS FORD**
> I your lady, Sir John! Alas, I should be a pitiful lady!

**FALSTAFF** *(rises up and crosses in front of downstage table, gesticulating and speaking with flourishes)*
> Let the court of France show me such another.
> I see how thine eye would emulate the diamond, and the firm fixture of thy foot would give an excellent motion to thy gait in a semi-circled farthingale. *(twirls around as if he is modeling a dress)*

**MISTRESS FORD** *(moves to table and sits on it seductively with*
*her legs crossed)*
Believe me, there is no such thing in me.

**FALSTAFF** *(still on his knees, sidles up next to her, trying to get close)*
What made me love thee? let that persuade thee
there's something extraordinary in thee. I love thee;
none but thee; and thou deservest it.

**MISTRESS FORD**
Do not betray me, sir. I fear you love Mistress Page.

**MISTRESS FORD** *moves abruptly toward the stage left chair, caus-*
*ing* **FALSTAFF** *to lose his balance and practically fall down, clutch-*
*ing frantically at the table to regain his balance.*

**FALSTAFF**
Thou mightst as well say I love to walk by the
Counter-gate, which is as hateful to me as the reek
of a lime-kiln.

**MISTRESS FORD**
Well, heaven knows how I love you;
and you shall one day find it.

**FALSTAFF**
Keep in that mind; I'll deserve it.

**FALSTAFF** *is excited so he mops his brow with a piece of laundry*
*from the basket. Suddenly he smells something—his armpits! He*
*frantically mops them with the piece of laundry and then throws*
*it back in the basket.*

*Enter* **ROBIN** *from stage left, still fussing with his glasses. He*
*addresses* **FALSTAFF**, *mistaking him for* **MISTRESS FORD**.

**ROBIN**

Mistress Ford!

FALSTAFF *moves* ROBIN *toward* MISTRESS FORD.

Mistress Ford! Here's Mistress Page at the door, sweating and blowing and looking wildly, and would needs speak with you presently.

**FALSTAFF**

She shall not see me. *(hides behind stage right pillar)*

*Exit* ROBIN *stage left just as* MISTRESS PAGE *enters stage left. They nearly bump into each other.*

**MISTRESS FORD** *(acting surprised)*

What's the matter? How now?

**MISTRESS PAGE** *(overacting)*

O Mistress Ford, what have you done? You're shamed, you're overthrown, you're undone for ever!

**MISTRESS FORD**

Why, alas, what's the matter?

**MISTRESS PAGE**

Your husband's coming hither, woman, with all the officers in Windsor, to search for a gentleman that he says is here now in the house by your consent: you are undone. If you have a friend here convey, convey him out. Defend your reputation, or bid farewell to your good life for ever. *(can hardly keep from laughing but continue their dialogue)*

**MISTRESS FORD**

What shall I do? There is a gentleman my dear

friend; and I fear not mine own shame so much as his peril.

**MISTRESS PAGE**

Bethink you of some conveyance: in the house you cannot hide him. Look, here is a basket: if he be of any reasonable stature, he may creep in here; and throw foul linen upon him—send him by your two men to Datchet-mead.

MISTRESS FORD *whistles and* SERVANTS *enter from stage right, still having their laundry fight.*

**MISTRESS FORD**

He's too big to go in there. What shall I do?

**FALSTAFF** *(coming forward)*

Let me see't, let me see't, O, let me see't! I'll in, I'll in. *(gets in the basket)*

**FALSTAFF** *(voice becomes muffled as* SERVANTS *cover him with dirty laundry)*

I love thee. Help me away. Let me creep in here. I'll never mmmphmmggg . . .

**MISTRESS FORD** *(to* SERVANTS*)*

Go take up these clothes here quickly.

SERVANTS *move in opposite directions, one going stage left and the other upstage.*

Look, how you drumble! Carry them to the laundress in Datchet-mead; quickly, come.

SERVANTS *start to exit stage left, pulling and pushing* FALSTAFF *in the basket.* MISTRESS FORD *and* MISTRESS PAGE *sit, quickly primping and preparing.*

*Enter* FORD, PAGE, SIR HUGH EVANS, *and* DOCTOR CAIUS *from stage left.*

SERVANTS *freeze.*

**FORD** *(to his group)*
> Pray you, come near: if I suspect without cause,
> why then make sport at me; then let me be your jest;
> I deserve it. *(to* SERVANTS*)* How now! Whither bear
> you this?

**SERVANT**
> To the laundress, forsooth.

*Exit* SERVANTS *stage left, hastily, as* MISTRESS FORD *shoos them off.*

**MISTRESS FORD** *(a little nervous)*
> Why, what have you to do whither they bear it? You
> were best meddle with buck-washing.

**FORD** *(sniffing around angrily like a mad hound dog)*
> Buck! I would I could wash myself of the buck! Buck,
> buck, buck! Ay, buck; I warrant you, buck; and of
> the season too, it shall appear. *(to his group)* Search,
> seek, find out: I'll warrant we'll unkennel the fox.
> You shall see sport anon: follow me, gentlemen.

*Exit* FORD *stage right.*

**SIR HUGH EVANS**
> This is fery fantastical humors and jealousies.

**DOCTOR CAIUS**
> By gar, 'tis no the fashion of France; it is not jealous

in France. (*does a little fake fencing toward* SIR HUGH, *who recoils in disgust*)

**PAGE**

Nay, follow him, gentlemen; see the issue of his search.

*Exit* PAGE, SIR HUGH EVANS, *and* DOCTOR CAIUS *stage right.*

**MISTRESS PAGE** (*laughing with* MISTRESS FORD)

Is there not a double excellency in this?

**MISTRESS FORD**

I know not which pleases me better; that my husband is deceived, or Sir John.

*Enter* FORD, PAGE, SIR HUGH EVANS, *and* DOCTOR CAIUS *from stage right.*

**FORD**

I cannot find him.

**DOCTOR CAIUS**

By gar, nor I too: there is no bodies.

**PAGE**

Fie, fie, Master Ford! Are you not ashamed?
What spirit, what devil suggests this imagination?

**FORD**

'Tis my fault, Master Page: I suffer for it.

**SIR HUGH EVANS**

You suffer for a pad conscience: your wife is
as honest a 'omans as I will desires among five
thousand, and five hundred too.

**DOCTOR CAIUS** *(looking her over and agreeing)*
> By gar, I see 'tis an honest woman.

**FORD** *(embarrassed; takes his wife's hand as she turns away in*
> *fake annoyance)*
> I pray you, pardon me. Come, wife; come, Mistress
> Page. I pray you, pardon me; pray heartily, pardon me.

MISTRESS PAGE *and* MISTRESS FORD *turn away, coyly teasing the*
*men by pretending to be offended and insulted.*

**PAGE**
> Let's go in, gentlemen; but, trust me, we'll mock
> him. Shall it be so?

**SIR HUGH EVANS**
> If there is one, I shall make two in the company.

**DOCTOR CAIUS**
> If dere be one or two, I shall make-a the turd.

**SIR HUGH EVANS**
> I pray you now, remembrance tomorrow on the
> lousy knave. A lousy knave, to have his gibes and
> his mockeries!

*Exit* ALL *stage rear.*

# ✳ **SCENE 3.** (ACT V, SCENE V)

*Windsor Forest.*

**STAGEHANDS** *remove table and chairs and hang leaves on pillars.*

*Enter* **NARRATOR** *from stage rear, coming downstage left.*

**NARRATOR**

> The Merry Wives have convinced Falstaff to dress up as Herne the Hunter, a folk hero who has antlers on his head. They promise to meet him in the woods, where many of our players have disguised themselves as fairies to have their comeuppance on the fat fool Falstaff.

*Exit* **NARRATOR** *stage left.*

*Enter* **FALSTAFF** *from stage rear.*

**SOUND OPERATOR** *plays* Sound Cue #1 *("Forest sounds").*

*Enter* **FALSTAFF** *from stage rear, disguised as Herne the Hunter. He stands center stage, looking around in awe and excitement. He is drunk with anticipation.*

**FALSTAFF**

> The Windsor bell hath struck twelve; the minute draws on. Now, the hot-blooded gods assist me! O powerful love! That, in some respects, makes a beast a man, in some other, a man a beast. O omnipotent Love! For me, I am here a Windsor stag; and the fattest, I think, i' the forest. Send me a cool rut-time,

Jove, or who can blame me to piss my tallow? Who comes here? My doe?

*Enter* MISTRESS FORD *from stage left.*

**MISTRESS FORD**

Sir John! Art thou there, my deer? My male deer? *(caresses his antlers)*

**FALSTAFF**

My doe with the black scut! Let the sky rain potatoes; let there come a tempest of provocation, I will shelter me here.

**MISTRESS FORD**

Mistress Page is come with me, sweetheart.

*Enter* MISTRESS PAGE *stage left. She and* MISTRESS FORD *place themselves on either side of* FALSTAFF, *and he puts his arms around them. It is his great moment of pleasure!*

**FALSTAFF**

Divide me like a bribe buck, each a haunch: Am I a woodman, ha? Speak I like Herne the hunter? As I am a true spirit, welcome!

SOUND OPERATOR *plays* Sound Cue #2 *("Fairy music and drumbeats").*

**MISTRESS PAGE**

Alas, what noise?

**MISTRESS FORD**

Heaven forgive our sins

**FALSTAFF**

What should this be?

**MISTRESS FORD** AND **MISTRESS PAGE**
>Away, away!

*Exit* MISTRESS FORD *and* MISTRESS PAGE *stage left, hurriedly.*

*Enter* MISTRESS QUICKLY, FORD *(with drum),* PAGE, DR. CAIUS,
SIR HUGH EVANS *(disguised with mask), and* PISTOL *(as Hobgoblin)*
*from stage right. Others, as* FAIRIES, *also enter from stage right,*
*following* MISTRESS QUICKLY, *who dances across the stage with her*
*wand and directs them to form a semicircle behind* FALSTAFF.

**MISTRESS QUICKLY**
>Fairies, black, grey, green, and white,
>You moonshine revellers and shades of night,
>You orphan heirs of fixed destiny,
>Attend your office and your quality.

**FALSTAFF**
>They are fairies; he that speaks to them shall die:
>I'll wink and couch: no man their works must eye.
>>*(lies face-down on the ground)*

**MISTRESS QUICKLY**
>About, about;
>Search Windsor Castle, elves, within and out:
>And "Honi soit qui mal y pense" write
>In emerald tufts, flowers purple, blue and white;
>Our dance of custom round about the oak
>Of Herne the hunter, let us not forget.

**SIR HUGH EVANS**
>Pray you, lock hand in hand; *(ALL join hands and*
>*start to circle around* FALSTAFF*)* yourselves in order set
>And twenty glow-worms shall our lanterns be,
>To guide our measure round about the tree.
>>*(circle divides to form a semicircle behind*
>>FALSTAFF *again;* SIR HUGH *sniffs at the air)*

But, stay; I smell a man of middle-earth.

**FALSTAFF**

Heavens defend me from that Welsh fairy, lest he
transform me to a piece of cheese!

**PISTOL** *(lunging at him)*

Vile worm, thou wast o'erlook'd even in thy birth.

**MISTRESS QUICKLY**

With trial-fire touch me his finger-end:
If he be chaste, the flame will back descend
And turn him to no pain; but if he start,
It is the flesh of a corrupted heart.

**PISTOL**

A trial, come.

**ALL** *lunge at* **FALSTAFF**, *fiercely yelling, "Aaaaaah!"*

**FALSTAFF**

Oh, Oh, Oh!

**MISTRESS QUICKLY**

Corrupt, corrupt, and tainted in desire!
About him, fairies; sing a scornful rhyme;
And, as you trip, still pinch him to your time.

*In the song that follows, characters sing individual lines. On bold
words,* **ALL** *sing and point at* **FALSTAFF**.

**MISTRESS QUICKLY**

**Fie** on sinful fantasy!
**Fie** on lust and luxury!

**FORD**

Lust is but a bloody fire,
Kindled with unchaste desire,

**SERVANT**

Fed in heart, whose flames aspire
As thoughts do blow them, higher and higher.

**DR. CAIUS**

Pinch him, fairies, mutually; *(they pinch him)*
Pinch him for his villany;

**SIR HUGH EVANS**

Pinch him, and burn him, and turn him about,
Till candles and starlight and moonshine be out!

ALL *lunge at* FALSTAFF, *yelling "Aaaaaah!" until he is shivering, cringing, and near tears.*

**MISTRESS PAGE** *(taking pity and compassion on him)*
I pray you, come, hold up the jest no higher.
*(takes off her mask)*
Now, good Sir John, how like you Windsor wives?

**FORD** *(takes off his mask)*
Now, sir, who's a cuckold now? Falstaff's a knave, a
cuckoldly knave; here are his horns, he hath enjoyed
nothing of Ford's but his buck-basket!

**MISTRESS FORD** *(takes off her mask)*
Sir John, we have had ill luck; we could never meet.
I will never take you for my love again; but I will
always count you my deer.

**FALSTAFF**

I do begin to perceive that I am made an ass.

**FORD**

> Ay, and an ox too: both the proofs are extant.

**FALSTAFF**

> And these are not fairies? *(FAIRIES remove their
> masks and laugh)* Well, I am your theme: you have
> the start of me; I am dejected; use me as you will.
> *(bows his head in shame and humility)*

**PAGE** *(helps him up)*

> Yet be cheerful, knight: thou shalt eat a posset
> tonight at my house; where I will desire thee to
> laugh at my wife, that now laughs at thee.

**FORD**

> Stand not amazed; here is no remedy:
> In love the heavens themselves do guide the state;
> Money buys lands, and wives are sold by fate.

**FALSTAFF**

> I am glad, though you have ta'en a special stand to
> strike at me, that your arrow hath glanced.

**MISTRESS PAGE**

> Well, I will muse no further.
> Heaven give you many, many merry days!
> Good husband, let us every one go home,
> And laugh this sport o'er by a country fire;
> Sir John and all. *(laughs as others join in)*

*All hold hands and take a bow. Exeunt.*

# ✳ PERFORMING SHAKESPEARE

## HOW *THE 30-MINUTE SHAKESPEARE* WAS BORN

In 1981 I performed a "Shakespeare Juggling" piece called "To Juggle or Not To Juggle" at the first Folger Library Secondary School Shakespeare Festival. The audience consisted of about 200 Washington, D.C. area high school students who had just performed thirty-minute versions of Shakespeare plays for each other and were jubilant over the experience. I was dressed in a jester's outfit, and my job was to entertain them. I juggled and jested and played with Shakespeare's words, notably Hamlet's "To be or not to be" soliloquy, to very enthusiastic response. I was struck by how much my "Shakespeare Juggling" resonated with a group who had just performed Shakespeare themselves. "Getting" Shakespeare is a heady feeling, especially for adolescents, and I am continually delighted at how much joy and satisfaction young people derive from performing Shakespeare. Simply reading and studying this great playwright does not even come close to inspiring the kind of enthusiasm that comes from performance.

Surprisingly, many of these students were not "actor types." A good percentage of the students performing Shakespeare that day were part of an English class which had rehearsed the plays during class time. Fifteen years later, when I first started directing plays in D.C. public schools as a Teaching Artist with the Folger Shakespeare Library, I entered a ninth grade English class as a guest and spent two or three days a week for two or three months preparing students for the Folger's annual Secondary School Shakespeare Festival. I have conducted this annual residency with the Folger ever since. Every year for seven action-packed days, eight groups of students between grades seven and twelve tread the boards onstage at the Folger's Elizabethan Theatre, a grand recreation of a sixteenth-century venue with a three-tiered gallery, carved oak columns, and a sky-painted canopy.

As noted on the Folger website (www.folger.edu), "The festival is a celebration of the Bard, not a competition. Festival commentators—drawn from the professional theater and Shakespeare education communities—recognize exceptional performances, student directors, and good spirit amongst the students with selected awards at the end of each day. They are also available to share feedback with the students."

My annual Folger Teaching Artist engagement, directing a Shakespeare play in a public high school English class, is the most challenging and the most rewarding thing I do all year. I hope this book can bring you the same rewards.

## GETTING STARTED

### GAMES

How can you get an English class (or any other group of young people, or even adults) to start the seemingly daunting task of performing a Shakespeare play? You have already successfully completed the critical first step, which is buying this book. You hold in your hand a performance-ready, thirty-minute cutting of a Shakespeare play, with stage directions to get the actors moving about the stage purposefully. But it's a good idea to warm the group up with some theater games.

One good initial exercise is called "Positive/Negative Salutations." Students stand in two lines facing each other (four or five students in each line) and, reading from index cards, greet each other, first with a "Positive" salutation in Shakespeare's language (using actual phrases from the plays), followed by a "negative" greeting.

Additionally, short vocal exercises are an essential part of the preparation process. The following is a very simple and effective vocal warm-up: Beginning with the number two, have the whole group count to twenty using increments of two (i.e., "Two, four, six . . ."). Increase the volume slightly with each number, reaching top volume with "twenty," and then decrease the volume while counting back down, so that the students are practically whispering when they arrive again at "two." This exercise teaches dynamics and allows them to get loud as a group without any individual pressure. Frequently during a rehearsal period, if a student is mumbling inaudibly, I will refer back to this exercise as a reminder that we can and often do belt it out!

"Stomping Words" is a game that is very helpful at getting a handle on Shakespeare's rhythm. Choose a passage in iambic pentameter and have the group members walk around the room in a circle, stomping their feet on the second beat of each line:

Two **house**-holds, **both** a-**like** in **dig**-nity
In **fair** Ve-**ro**na **Where** we **lay** our **scene**

Do the same thing with a prose passage, and have the students discuss their experience with it, including points at which there is an extra beat, etc., and what, if anything, it might signify.

I end every vocal warm-up with a group reading of one of the speeches from the play, emphasizing diction and projection, bouncing off consonants, and encouraging the group members to listen to each other so that they can speak the lines together in unison. For variety I will throw in some classic "tongue twisters" too, such as, "The sixth sheik's sixth sheep is sick."

The Folger Shakespeare Library's website (http://www.folger.edu) and their book series *Shakespeare Set Free,* edited by Peggy O'Brien, are two great resources for getting started with a performance-based teaching of Shakespeare in the classroom. The Folger website has numerous helpful resources and activities, many submitted by teachers, for helping a class actively participate in the process of getting to know a Shakespeare play. For more simple theater games, Viola Spolin's *Theatre Games for the Classroom* is very helpful, as is one I use frequently, *Theatre Games for Young Performers.*

## HATS AND PROPS

Introducing a few hats and props early in the process is a good way to get the action going. Hats, in particular, provide a nice avenue for giving young actors a non-verbal way of getting into character. In the opening weeks, when students are still holding onto their scripts, a hat can give an actor a way to "feel" like a character. Young actors are natural masters at injecting their own personality into what they wear, and even small choices made with how a hat is worn (jauntily, shadily, cockily, mysteriously) provide a starting point for discussion of specific characters, their traits, and their relationships with other characters. All such discussions always lead back to one thing: the text. "Mining the text" is consistently the best strategy for uncovering the mystery of Shakespeare's language. That is where all the answers lie: in the words themselves.

## WHAT DO THE WORDS MEAN?

It is essential that young actors know what they are saying when they recite Shakespeare. If not, they might as well be scat singing, riffing on sounds and rhythm but not conveying a specific meaning. The real question is: What do the words mean? The answer is multifaceted, and can be found in more than one place. The New Folger Library paperback editions of the plays themselves (edited by Barbara Mowat and Paul Werstine, Washington Square Press) are a great resource for understanding Shakespeare's words and passages and "translating" them into modern English. These editions also contain chapters on Shakespeare's language, his life, his theater, a "Modern Perspective," and further reading. There is a wealth of scholarship embedded in these wonderful books, and I make it a point to read them cover to cover before embarking on a play-directing project. At the very least, it is a good idea for any adult who intends to direct a Shakespeare play with a group of students to go through the explanatory notes that appear on the pages facing the text. These explanatory notes are an indispensable "translation tool."

The best way to get students to understand what Shakespeare's words mean is to ask them what they think they mean. Students have their own associations with the words and with how they sound and feel. The best ideas on how to perform Shakespeare often come directly from the students, not from anybody else's notion. If a student has an idea or feeling about a word or passage, and it resonates with her emotionally, physically, or spiritually, then Shakespeare's words can be a vehicle for her feelings. That can result in some powerful performances!

I make it my job as director to read the explanatory notes in the Folger text, but I make it clear to the students that almost "anything goes" when trying to understand Shakespeare. There are no wrong interpretations. Students have their own experiences, with some shared and some uniquely their own. If someone has an association with the phrase "canker-blossom," or if the words make that student or his character feel or act a certain way, then that is the "right" way to decipher it.

I encourage the students to refer to the Folger text's explanatory notes and to keep a pocket dictionary handy. Young actors must attach some meaning to every word or line they recite. If I feel an actor is glossing over a word, I will stop him and ask him what he is saying. If he doesn't know, we will figure it out together as a group.

## PROCESS VS. PRODUCT

The process of learning Shakespeare by performing one of his plays is more important than whether everybody remembers his lines or whether somebody misses a cue or an entrance. But my Teaching Artist residencies have always had the end goal of a public performance for about 200 other students, so naturally the performance starts to take precedence over the process somewhere around dress rehearsal in the students' minds. It is my job to make sure the actors are prepared—otherwise they will remember the embarrassing moment of a public mistake and not the glorious triumph of owning a Shakespeare play.

In one of my earlier years of play directing, I was sitting in the audience as one of my narrators stood frozen on stage for at least a minute, trying to remember her opening line. I started scrambling in my backpack below my seat for a script, at last prompting her from the audience. Despite her fine performance, that embarrassing moment is all she remembered from the whole experience. Since then I have made sure to assign at least one person to prompt from backstage if necessary. Additionally, I inform the entire cast that if somebody is dying alone out there, it is okay to rescue him or her with an offstage prompt.

There is always a certain amount of stage fright that will accompany a performance, especially a public one for an unfamiliar audience. As a director, I live with stage fright as well, even though I am not appearing on stage. The only antidote to this is work and preparation. If a young actor is struggling with her lines, I make sure to arrange for a session where we run lines over the telephone. I try to set up a buddy system so that students can run lines with their peers, and this often works well. But if somebody does not have a "buddy," I will personally make the time to help out myself. As I assure my students from the outset, I am not going to let them fail or embarrass themselves. They need an experienced leader. And if the leader has experience in teaching but not in directing Shakespeare, then he needs this book!

It is a good idea to culminate in a public performance, as opposed to an in-class project, even if it is only for another classroom. Student actors want to show their newfound Shakespearian thespian skills to an outside group, and this goal motivates them to do a good job. In that respect, "product" is important. Another wonderful bonus to performing a play is that it is a unifying group effort. Students learn teamwork. They learn to give focus to another actor when he is

speaking, and to play off of other characters. I like to end each performance with the entire cast reciting a passage in unison. This is a
powerful ending, one that reaffirms the unity of the group.

## SEEING SHAKESPEARE PERFORMED

It is very helpful for young actors to see Shakespeare performed by
a group of professionals, whether they are appearing live on stage
(preferable but not always possible) or on film. Because an entire play
can take up two or more full class periods, time may be an issue. I am
fortunate because thanks to a local foundation that underwrites theater
education in the schools, I have been able to take my school groups
to a Folger Theatre matinee of the play that they are performing. I
always pick a play that is being performed locally that season. But
not all group leaders are that lucky. Fortunately, there is the Internet,
specifically YouTube. A quick YouTube search for "Shakespeare" can
unearth thousands of results, many appropriate for the classroom.

The first "Hamlet" result showed an 18-year-old African-American
actor on the streets of Camden, New Jersey, delivering a riveting
performance of Hamlet's "The play's the thing." The second clip was
from *Cat Head Theatre,* an animation of cats performing Hamlet.
Of course, YouTube boasts not just alley cats and feline thespians,
but also clips by true legends of the stage, such as John Gielgud and
Richard Burton. These clips can be saved and shown in classrooms,
providing useful inspiration.

One advantage of the amazing variety of clips available on YouTube
is that students can witness the wide range of interpretations for any
given scene, speech, or character in Shakespeare, thus freeing them
from any preconceived notion that there is a "right" way to do it.
Furthermore, modern interpretations of the Bard may appeal to those
who are put off by the "thees and thous" of Elizabethan speech.

By seeing Shakespeare performed either live or on film, students
are able to hear the cadence, rhythm, vocal dynamics, and pronuncia-
tion of the language, and they can appreciate the life that other actors

breathe into the characters. They get to see the story told dramatically, which inspires them to tell their own version.

## PUTTING IT ALL TOGETHER

### THE STEPS

After a few sessions of theater games to warm up the group, it's time to begin the process of casting the play. Each play cutting in *The 30-Minute Shakespeare* series includes a cast list and a sample program, demonstrating which parts have been divided. Cast size is generally between twelve and thirty students, with major roles frequently assigned to more than one performer. In other words, one student may play Juliet in the first scene, another in the second scene, and yet another in the third. This will distribute the parts evenly so that there is no "star of the show." Furthermore, this prevents actors from being burdened with too many lines. If I have an actor who is particularly talented or enthusiastic, I will give her a bigger role. It is important to go with the grain—one cast member's enthusiasm can be contagious.

I provide the performer of each shared role with a similar head-piece and/or cape, so that the audience can keep track of the characters. When there are sets of twins, I try to use blue shirts and red shirts, so that the audience has at least a fighting chance of figuring it out! Other than these costume consistencies, I rely on the text and the audience's observance to sort out the doubling of characters. Generally, the audience can follow because we are telling the story.

Some participants are shy and do not wish to speak at all on stage. To these students I assign non-speaking parts and technical roles such as sound operator and stage manager. However, I always get everybody on stage at some point, even if it is just for the final group speech, because I want every group member to experience what it is like to be on a stage as part of an ensemble.

## CASTING THE PLAY

Young people can be self-conscious and nervous with "formal" auditions, especially if they have little or no acting experience.

I conduct what I call an "informal" audition process. I hand out a questionnaire asking students if there is any particular role that they desire, whether they play a musical instrument. To get a feel for them as people, I also ask them to list one or two hobbies or interests. Occasionally this will inform my casting decisions. If someone can juggle, and the play has the part of a Fool, that skill may come in handy. Dancing or martial arts abilities can also be applied to roles.

For the auditions, I do not use the cut script. I have students stand and read from the Folger edition of the complete text in order to hear how they fare with the longer passages. I encourage them to breathe and carry their vocal energy all the way to the end of a long line of text. I also urge them to play with diction, projection, modulation, and dynamics, elements of speech that we have worked on in our vocal warm-ups and theater games.

I base my casting choices largely on reading ability, vocal strength, and enthusiasm for the project. If someone has requested a particular role, I try to honor that request. I explain that even with a small part, an actor can create a vivid character that adds a lot to the play. Wide variations in personality types can be utilized: if there are two students cast as Romeo, one brooding and one effusive, I try to put the more brooding Romeo in an early lovelorn scene, and place the effusive Romeo in the balcony scene. Occasionally one gets lucky, and the doubling of characters provides a way to match personality types with different aspects of a character's personality. But also be aware of the potential serendipity of non-traditional casting. For example, I have had one of the smallest students in the class play a powerful Othello. True power comes from within!

Generally, I have more females than males in a class, so women are more likely (and more willing) to play male characters than vice versa.

Rare is the high school boy who is brave enough to play a female character, which is unfortunate because it can reap hilarious results.

## GET OUTSIDE HELP

Every time there is a fight scene in one of the plays I am directing, I call on my friend Michael Tolaydo, a professional actor and theater professor at St. Mary's College, who is an expert in all aspects of theater, including fight choreography. Not only does Michael stage the fight, but he does so in a way that furthers the action of the play, highlighting character's traits and bringing out the best in the student actors. Fight choreography must be done by an expert or somebody could get hurt. In the absence of such help, super slow-motion fights are always a safe bet and can be quite effective, especially when accompanied by a soundtrack on the boom box.

During dress rehearsals I invite my friend Hilary Kacser. a Washington-area actor and dialect coach for two decades. Because I bring her in late in the rehearsal process, I have her direct her comments to me, which I then filter and relay to the cast. This avoids confusing the cast with a second set of directions. This caveat only applies to general directorial comments from outside visitors. Comments on specific artistic disciplines such as dance, music, and stage combat can come from the outside experts themselves.

If you work in a school, you might have helpful resources within your own building, such as a music or dance teacher who could contribute their expertise to a scene. If nobody is available in your school, try seeking out a member of the local professional theater. Many local performing artists will be glad to help, and the students are usually thrilled to have a visit from a professional performer.

## LET STUDENTS BRING THEMSELVES INTO THE PLAY

The best ideas often come from the students themselves. If a young actor has a notion of how to play a scene, I will always give that idea a try. In a rehearsal of *Henry IV, Part 1,* one traveler jumped into the other's arms when they were robbed. It got a huge laugh. This was something that they did on instinct. We kept that bit for the performance, and it worked wonderfully.

As a director, you have to foster an environment in which that kind of spontaneity can occur. The students have to feel safe to experiment. In the same production of *Henry IV*, Falstaff and Hal invented a little fist bump "secret handshake" to use in the battle scene. The students were having fun and bringing parts of themselves into the play. Shakespeare himself would have approved. When possible I try to err on the side of fun because if the young actors are having fun, then they will commit themselves to the project. The beauty of the language, the story, the characters, and the pathos will follow.

There is a balance to be achieved here, however. In that same production of *Henry IV, Part 1*, the student who played Bardolph was having a great time with her character. She carried a leather wineskin around and offered it up to the other characters in the tavern. It was a prop with which she developed a comic relationship. At the end of our thirty-minute *Henry IV, Part 1*, I added a scene from *Henry IV, Part 2* as a coda: The new King Henry V (formerly Falstaff's drinking and carousing buddy Hal) rejects Falstaff, banishing him from within ten miles of the King. It is a sad and sobering moment, one of the most powerful in the play.

But at the performance, in the middle of the King's rejection speech (played by a female student, and her only speech), Bardolph offered her flask to King Henry and got a big laugh, thus not only upstaging the King but also undermining the seriousness and poignancy of the whole scene. She did not know any better; she was bringing herself to the character as I had been encouraging her to do. But it was inappropriate, and in subsequent seasons, if I foresaw something like that happening as an individual joyfully occupied a character, I attempted to prevent it. Some things we cannot predict. Now I make sure to issue a statement warning against changing any of the blocking on show day, and to watch out for upstaging one's peers.

## FOUR FORMS OF ENGAGEMENT: VOCAL, EMOTIONAL, PHYSICAL, AND INTELLECTUAL

When directing a Shakespeare play with a group of students, I always start with the words themselves because the words have the power to engage the emotions, mind, and body. Also, I start with the words in action, as in the previously mentioned exercise, "Positive and Negative Salutations." Students become physically engaged; their bodies react to the images the words evoke. The words have the power to trigger a switch in both the teller and the listener, eliciting both an emotional and physical reaction. I have never heard a student utter the line "Fie! Fie! You counterfeit, you puppet you!" without seeing him change before my eyes. His spine stiffens, his eyes widen, and his fingers point menacingly.

Having used Shakespeare's words to engage the students emotionally and physically, one can then return to the text for a more reflective discussion of what the words mean to us personally. I always make sure to leave at least a few class periods open for discussion of the text, line by line, to ensure that students understand intellectually what they feel viscerally. The advantage to a performance-based teaching of Shakespeare is that by engaging students vocally, emotionally, and physically, it is then much easier to engage them intellectually because they are invested in the words, the characters, and the story. We always start on our feet, and later we sit and talk.

## SIX ELEMENTS OF DRAMA: PLOT, CHARACTER, THEME, DICTION, MUSIC, AND SPECTACLE

Over two thousand years ago, Aristotle's *Poetics* outlined six elements of drama, in order of importance: Plot, Character, Theme, Diction, Music, and Spectacle. Because Shakespeare was foremost a playwright, it is helpful to take a brief look at these six elements as they relate to directing a Shakespeare play in the classroom.

## PLOT (ACTION)

To Aristotle, plot was the most important element. One of the purposes of *The 30-Minute Shakespeare* is to provide a script that tells Shakespeare's stories, as opposed to concentrating on one scene. In a thirty-minute edit of a Shakespeare play, some plot elements are necessarily omitted. For the sake of a full understanding of the characters' relationships and motivations, it is helpful to make short plot summaries of each scene so that students are aware of their characters' arcs throughout the play. The scene descriptions in the Folger editions are sufficient to fill in the plot holes. Students can read the descriptions aloud during class time to ensure that the story is clear and that no plot elements are neglected. Additionally, there are one-page charts in the Folger editions of *Shakespeare Set Free,* indicating characters' relations graphically, with lines connecting families and factions to give students a visual representation of what can often be complex interrelationships, particularly in Shakespeare's history plays.

Young actors love action. That is why *The 30-Minute Shakespeare* includes dynamic blocking (stage direction) that allows students to tell the story in a physically dramatic fashion. Characters' movements on the stage are always motivated by the text itself.

## CHARACTER

I consider myself a facilitator and a director more than an acting teacher. I want the students' understanding of their characters to spring from the text and the story. From there, I encourage them to consider how their character might talk, walk, stand, sit, eat, and drink. I also urge students to consider characters' motivations, objectives, and relationships, and I will ask pointed questions to that end during the rehearsal process. I try not to show the students how I would perform a scene, but if no ideas are forthcoming from anybody in the class, I will suggest a minimum of two possibilities for how the character might respond.

At times students may want more guidance and examples. Over thirteen years of directing plays in the classroom, I have wavered between wanting all the ideas to come from the students, and deciding that I need to be more of a "director," telling them what I would like to see them doing. It is a fine line, but in recent years I have decided that if I don't see enough dynamic action or characterization, I will step in and "direct" more. But I always make sure to leave room for students to bring themselves into the characters because their own ideas are invariably the best.

## THEME (THOUGHTS, IDEAS)

In a typical English classroom, theme will be a big topic for discussion of a Shakespeare play. Using a performance-based method of teaching Shakespeare, an understanding of the play's themes develops from "mining the text" and exploring Shakespeare's words and his story. If the students understand what they are saying and how that relates to their characters and the overall story, the plays' themes will emerge clearly. We always return to the text itself. There are a number of elegant computer programs, such as www.wordle.net, that will count the number of recurring words in a passage and illustrate them graphically. For example, if the word "jealousy" comes up more than any other word in *Othello,* it will appear in a larger font. Seeing the words displayed by size in this way can offer up illuminating insights into the interaction between words in the text and the play's themes. Your computer-minded students might enjoy searching for such tidbits. There are more internet tools and websites in the Additional Resources section at the back of this book.

I cannot overstress the importance of acting out the play in understanding its themes. By embodying the roles of Othello and Iago and reciting their words, students do not simply comprehend the themes intellectually, but understand them kinesthetically, physically, and emotionally. They are essentially *living* the characters' jealousy, pride, and feelings about race. The themes of appearance vs.

reality, good vs. evil, honesty, misrepresentation, and self-knowledge (or lack thereof) become physically felt as well as intellectually understood. Performing Shakespeare delivers a richer understanding than that which comes from just reading the play. Students can now relate the characters' conflicts to their own struggles.

## DICTION (LANGUAGE)

If I had to cite one thing I would like my actors to take from their experience of performing a play by William Shakespeare, it is an appreciation and understanding of the beauty of Shakespeare's language. The language is where it all begins and ends. Shakespeare's stories are dramatic, his characters are rich and complex, and his settings are exotic and fascinating, but it is through his language that these all achieve their richness. This leads me to spend more time on language than on any other element of the performance.

Starting with daily vocal warm-ups, many of them using parts of the script or other Shakespearean passages, I consistently emphasize the importance of the words. Young actors often lack experience in speaking clearly and projecting their voices outward, so in addition to comprehension, I emphasize projection, diction, breathing, pacing, dynamics, coloring of words, and vocal energy. *Theatre Games for Young Performers* contains many effective vocal exercises, as does the Folger's *Shakespeare Set Free* series. Consistent emphasis on all aspects of Shakespeare's language, especially on how to speak it effectively, is the most important element to any Shakespeare performance with a young cast.

## MUSIC

A little music can go a long way in setting a mood for a thirty-minute Shakespeare play. I usually open the show with a short passage of music to set the tone. Thirty seconds of music played on a boom box operated by a student can provide a nice introduction to the play, create an atmosphere for the audience, and give the actors a sense of place and feeling.

iTunes is a good starting point for choosing your music. Typing in "Shakespeare" or "Hamlet" or "jealousy" (if you are going for a theme) will result in an excellent selection of aural performance enhancers at the very reasonable price of ninety-nine cents each (or free of charge, see Additional Resources section). Likewise, fight sounds, foreboding sounds, weather sounds (rain, thunder), trumpet sounds, etc. are all readily available online at affordable cost. I typically include three sound cues in a play, just enough to enhance but not overpower a production. The boom box operator sits on the far right or left of the stage, not backstage, so he can see the action. This also has the added benefit of having somebody out there with a script, capable of prompting in a pinch.

## SPECTACLE

Aristotle considered spectacle the least important aspect of drama. Students tend to be surprised at this since we are used to being bombarded with production values on TV and video, often at the expense of substance. In my early days of putting on student productions, I would find myself hamstrung by my own ambitions in the realm of scenic design.

A simple bench or two chairs set on the stage are sufficient. The sense of "place" can be achieved through language and acting. Simple set dressing, a few key props, and some tasteful, emblematic costume pieces will go a long way toward providing all the "spectacle" you need.

In the stage directions to the plays in *The 30-Minute Shakespeare* series, I make frequent use of two large pillars stage left and right at the Folger Shakespeare Library's Elizabethan Theatre. I also have characters frequently entering and exiting from "stage rear." Your stage will have a different layout. Take a good look at the performing space you will be using and see if there are any elements that can be incorporated into your own stage directions. Is there a balcony? Can characters enter from the audience? (Make sure that they can get there from backstage, unless you want them waiting in the lobby until their entrance, which may be impractical.) If possible, make sure to rehearse in that space a few times to fix any technical issues and perhaps discover a few fun staging variations that will add pizzazz and dynamics to your own show.

The real spectacle is in the telling of the tale. Wooden swords are handy for characters that need them. Students should be warned at the outset that playing with swords outside of the scene is verboten. Letters, moneybags, and handkerchiefs should all have plentiful duplicates kept in a small prop box, as well as with a stage manager, because they tend to disappear in the hands of adolescents. After every rehearsal and performance, I recommend you personally sweep the rehearsal or performance area immediately for stray props. It is amazing what gets left behind.

Ultimately, the performances are about language and human drama, not set pieces, props, and special effects. Fake blood, glitter, glass, and liquids have no place on the stage; they are a recipe for disaster, or, at the very least, a big mess. On the other hand, the props that are employed can often be used effectively to convey character, as in Bardolph's aforementioned relationship with his wineskin.

## PITFALLS AND SOLUTIONS

Putting on a play in a high school classroom is not easy. There are problems with enthusiasm, attitude, attention, and line memorization, to name a few. As anybody who has directed a play will tell you, it is always darkest before the dawn. My experience is that after one or two days of utter despair just before the play goes up, show day breaks and the play miraculously shines. To quote a recurring gag in one of my favorite movies, *Shakespeare in Love:* "It's a mystery."

## ENTHUSIASM, FRUSTRATION, AND DISCIPLINE

Bring the enthusiasm yourself. Feed on the energy of the eager students, and others will pick up on that. Keep focused on the task at hand. Arrive prepared. Enthusiasm comes as you make headway. Ultimately, it helps to remind the students that a play is fun. I try to focus on the positive attributes of the students, rather than the ones that drive me crazy. This is easier said than done, but it is important. One season, I yelled at the group two days in a row. On day two of yelling, they tuned me out, and it took me a while to win them back. I learned my lesson; since then I've tried not to raise my voice out of anger or frustration. As I grow older and more mature, it is important for me to lead by example. It has been years since I yelled at a student group. If I am disappointed in their work or their behavior, I will express my disenchantment in words, speaking from the heart as somebody who cares about them and cares about our performance and our experience together. I find that fundamentally, young people want to please, to do well, and to be liked. If there is a serious discipline problem, I will hand it over to the regular classroom teacher, the administrator, or the parent.

## LINE MEMORIZATION

Students may have a hard time memorizing lines. In these cases, see if you can pair them up with a "buddy" and existing friend who will run lines with them in person or over the phone after school. If students do not have such a "buddy," I volunteer to run lines with them myself. If serious line memorization problems arise that cannot be solved through work, then two students can switch parts if it is early enough in the rehearsal process. For doubled roles, the scene with fewer lines can go to the actor who is having memorization problems. Additionally, a few passages or lines can be cut. Again, it is important to address these issues early. Later cuts become more problematic as other actors have already memorized their cues. I have had to do late cuts about twice in thirteen years. While they have gotten us out of jams, it is best to assess early whether a student will have line memorization problems, and deal with the problem sooner rather than later.

In production, always keep several copies of the script backstage, as well as cheat sheets indicating cues, entrances, and scene changes. Make a prop list, indicating props for each scene, as well as props that are the responsibility of individual actors. Direct the Stage Manager and an Assistant Stage Manager to keep track of these items, and on show days, personally double-check if you can.

In thirteen years of preparing an inner-city public high school English class for a public performance on a field trip to the Folger Secondary School Shakespeare Festival, my groups and I have been beset by illness, emotional turmoil, discipline problems, stage fright, adolescent angst, midlife crises (not theirs), and all manner of other emergencies, including acts of God and nature. Despite the difficulties and challenges inherent in putting on a Shakespeare play with a group of young people, one amazing fact stands out in my experience. Here is how many times a student has been absent for show day: Zero. Somehow, everybody has always made it to the show, and the show has gone on. How can this be? It's a mystery.

# ✳ PERFORMANCE NOTES: *THE MERRY WIVES OF WINDSOR*

Shakespeare's *The Merry Wives of Windsor* is dear to my heart, as I performed in the Folger Theatre's 1985 production of the play. The staging featured a circus motif, and I played Jack Rugby, servant to Dr. Caius, a small role that was transformed into a juggler's part to take advantage of my specific skills. Mistress Quickly was played in drag, Master and Mistress Ford in whiteface, and Master and Mistress Page as commedia dell'arte characters. Sir John Falstaff was a bumbling clown with big shoes and a red nose.

Although this 1998 production of *The Merry Wives of Windsor* was not circus-themed, I tried to keep that same spirit of mayhem in the performance. I was fortunate to have a ninth grader as Falstaff who embodied that character's infectious charm and self-adoring buffoonery. Falstaff's entourage, Pistol, Nym, and young Robin, are cartoonish in word and deed. With the addition of Sir Hugh Evans and Dr. Caius, who both make a joke out of the English language, the play provides hearty laughs in a madcap comedy.

These notes are the result of my own review of the performance video. They are not intended to be the "definitive" performance notes for all productions of *The Merry Wives of Windsor*. Your production will be unique to you and your cast. That is the magic of live theater. What is interesting about these notes is that many of the performance details I mention were not part of the original stage directions. They either emerged spontaneously on performance day or were developed by students in rehearsal after the stage directions had been written into the script. Some of these pieces of stage business work like a charm. Others fall flat. Still others are unintentionally hilarious. My favorites are the ones that arise directly from the students themselves and demonstrate a union between actor and character, as if that individual becomes a vehicle for the character he is playing. To witness a fifteen-year-old boy "become" Falstaff as Shakespeare's words leave his mouth is a memorable moment indeed.

## SCENE 1 (ACT I, SCENE III)

As the narrator introduces the first scene, the players cross the stage in character. This is effective for a number of reasons: it sets a fun tone while introducing the main characters to the audience, and it gives the actors themselves an opportunity to get into character. They must search for personality traits or mannerisms they can physicalize. The host enters whistling and polishing a mug, setting the mood (lighthearted) and the place (a tavern). Nym gives us a big, leaping "ta da" move with hyperextended arms and legs, whereas Pistol's body language is more rough and ornery as he jostles with Nym. Robin runs out childishly clutching a doll, wearing oversized glasses, and bumping into the pillar. Finally, Falstaff waddles onstage with a mischievous grin, holding his oversized belly. Audiences need to get their bearings during Shakespeare plays. The language is daunting for them, especially initially. By clarifying character traits and relationships early, sometimes through physical means, we can help the audience relax into the play, allowing the story and language to work their magic.

The actor playing Bardolph knew how to juggle. If a young performer has a special skill, try to find a place for it in the play. Bardolph is a drunk, so giving him juggling skills provides a delicious irony. On the line "It is a life that I have desired: I will thrive!" he stands on a chair, which adds a nice dimension to the staging. In performance, this moment was too short. The actor playing Bardolph stopped juggling and descended from the chair just as the audience applause was rising. Excessive haste is common among young actors, so they should be instructed not to step on their applause or laughter. Because most rehearsals are conducted with no onlookers present, it is helpful to have a small audience at some of the final rehearsals, giving performers a chance to adjust for laughter and other possible crowd responses.

Young actors can also be encouraged to look for breathing points in Shakespearean passages, as well as *beats,* or moments in a line that indicate a shift in the actor's thought, emotion, or action. Players can mark pauses and beats in their scripts, which will go a long way toward maintaining rhythm and pacing in their speeches. It will also help prevent them from running out of breath in the middle of a line!

This cast had a knack for grasping the comedic charm of the play, and they demonstrated this by executing their physical comedy bits with zest. Before Falstaff asks, "Which of you know Ford of this town?" he looks to his right and left (checking for eavesdroppers), and then huddles conspiratorially with Pistol and Nym, who also glance about nervously. These "pieces of business" bring the text to life, adding punch to the story itself. When Pistol exclaims, "Two yards and more" (referring to Falstaff's girth), Nym laughs—and keeps laughing until he notices he is the only one, wipes his mouth, and falls silent, embarrassed. Timing is tricky with this kind of gag, but the ninth-grade Nym pulled it off brilliantly, and she was rewarded with sustained laughter from the audience.

Even in a farcical romp, Shakespeare's language and characters are so rich that young actors can paint a colorful theatrical picture for the audience. Falstaff outlines his plan to seduce both Mistresses Ford and Page with the line, "They shall be my East and West Indies, and I will trade to them both." Our Falstaff takes a moment in which he imagines this conquest and tilts his head back with his eyes closed, rocking back and forth in his chair, lost in reverie. Nym snaps his fingers in Falstaff's face and he awakens with a start. Again, these two players timed it perfectly, and they rode a wave of audience laughter.

After years of performing and directing comedy, the reason why some gags work and some fail remains somewhat mysterious to me, but part of this gag's success was because it was *not rushed*. In fact, it went on a little longer than the audience expected, and that incongruity or surprise contributed to the laughter. Another factor is the *attention* the other students on stage gave their peer. As he drifted into his daydream, Pistol, Nym, and Robin leaned in a little and looked at him inquisitively. When all actors on the stage have the proper focus, theater magic happens.

I try to instill in my cast the importance of giving focus on stage. They must support their fellow actors by committing to the relationships and the drama. Only by actors' dedication to stage moments can the audience fully enter the world of the play. Fortunately, the student playing Falstaff was completely engrossed in his role. On the line, "Rogues, hence, avaunt!" he gestured so wildly that his hat flew off. He was so over the top that he surprised the audience into laughter. His enthusiasm was contagious.

The first scene ends with Pistol and Nym high-fiving each other after vowing revenge on Falstaff. They pause, look around nervously, then steal everything on the table (cups, forks, even the tablecloth) and run off. By the end of this scene, the audience is fully engaged and primed for more laughter. When it works, performing comedy can be very rewarding, especially in the hands of teenagers discovering Shakespeare for the first time.

## SCENE 2 (ACT III, SCENE III)

As in the first scene, the characters for Scene 2 walk across the stage as they are introduced. Mistress Ford and Mistress Page giggle conspiratorially. Master Ford wears a fake moustache and growls like a dog. Dr. Caius tosses his cape over his face with a flourish. In this production, the same actress who portrayed Nym doubled as Dr. Caius. She bravely adopted a ridiculous French accent, went for laughs, and got them! Laughter, like enthusiasm, is contagious. To quote Shakespeare's Nym, "The humor rises; it is good."

When Falstaff enters suavely to seduce Mistress Ford, he steps into the buck basket and gets his foot caught in it, a foreshadowing of his subsequent buck basket escapades. Part of comedy acting is keeping a keen eye out for potential running gags. Next I have Falstaff's foot get caught in the buck basket twice, and the third time his entire body becomes prey to it. The rule of three does work in comedy. Use it.

Proper blocking enhances visual humor. In this scene Falstaff is hiding under the table at Mistress Page's feet, looking straight out toward the audience, who can see the panic on Falstaff's face as he reacts to the news of Master Page's imminent arrival. To enhance the physical slapstick, our Falstaff develops a nervous facial twitch as his panic increases. Small details matter.

There are numerous language gags in *The Merry Wives of Windsor.* Pistol speaks in pirate-like bursts of colorful language ("Let vultures gripe thy guts!") and Nym uses the word "humor" in almost every sentence. The best example of linguistic funny business in this production came from Dr. Caius. In addition to a thick French accent, our young actress chose to place the accent on the wrong syllable when she spoke. Thus "*ho*-nest *wo*-man" became "ho-*nest* wo-*man*." This incongruity added another layer of absurdity to an already hilarious character.

## SCENE 3 (ACT V, SCENE V)

The scene changes in this play take place at breakneck speed, another component of presenting an entertaining and fast-paced show. I tell the actors that the stage should never be bare. As in a relay race, when one player exits, the other should be entering, so the action never breaks. Falstaff enters the final scene to New Age music, wearing a pair of deer antlers. He leads with his nose, prances and stamps, clearly reveling in his role. The audience squeals with delight.

As a member of the gang of fairies, Master Ford plays a large tom-tom drum. Following the accented syllables of the fairies' song, he leans in close to a cowering Falstaff and points at him accusingly with the drumstick. The assembled cast encircles Falstaff and menaces him with key words: "fie," "lust," "kindled," and "pinch." On the word "pinch," the group members lunge in and pinch poor Falstaff, who ends up lying on his back, writhing and spread-eagled on the stage. It is a dramatic stage picture, painted by the entire ensemble in unison.

This production was enacted by a group of ninth graders in a D.C. public school. Ninth graders are at the bottom of the high school totem pole, but after this group of freshmen used Shakespeare's beautiful language and colorful characters to perform his merry tale to a laughing, applauding audience, they were on top of the world. May this be your story too.

# ✳ *THE MERRY WIVES OF WINDSOR:* SET AND PROP LIST

SET PIECES:

Table
Five stools

PROPS:

**SCENE 1:**
Tablecloth
Candleholder
Candle
Bottle
Silverware
Mugs
Rag
Eyeglasses
Juggling balls
Two envelopes, one labled "Mistress Ford" and one labeled
     "Mistress Page"
Money purse

**SCENE 2:**
Purse containing comb and makeup
Laundry basket and laundry

**SCENE 3:**
Leaves
Deer antlers
Drums
Masks

Tuesday, March 26th, 1998

BENJAMIN BANNEKER ACADEMIC HIGH SCHOOL *presents*

# The Merry Wives of Windsor

## By William Shakespeare

Instructor: Mr. Leo Bowman | Guest Director: Mr. Nick Newlin

### CAST OF CHARACTERS:

**Sir John Falstaff:** Jason Murphy

**Mistress Ford:** Maria Eusebio

**Mistress Page:** Malaika Brown

**Pistol:** Shana Wilson

**Nym:** Maya Mapp

**Bardolph:** Jason Shine

**Host:** Asia Carter

**Ford:** Jarreau Barnes

**Page:** Melvin Moore

**Dr. Caius:** Maya Mapp

**Hugh Evans:** Maleka Smith

**Mistress Quickly:** Tiarra Kernan

**Robin:** Remel Thomas

**Servants:** Corinne Sampson and Nikia Brock

**Narrators:** Remel Thomas, Nikia Brock, Teal Cole

**Stage Manage:** Kunle Adenariwo

**Programs:** Allison Jones

**Sets, Props, Stagehands:** Victor Davis, Brandon Jenkins,
Allison Jones, Nikia Brock, Adar Howard, Shantay Fields,
Boc Kan Yee, Quyen Nguyen, Mercedes Edwards, Fatima Parker

*We'll use this unwholesome humidity,*
*this gross watery pumpion;*
*we'll teach him to know turtles from jays.*
Mistress Ford

# ADDITIONAL RESOURCES

## SHAKESPEARE

*Shakespeare Set Free: Teaching Romeo and Juliet, Macbeth and a Midsummer Night's Dream*
Peggy O'Brien, Ed., Teaching Shakespeare Institute
Washington Square Press
New York, 1993

*Shakespeare Set Free: Teaching Hamlet and Henry IV, Part 1*
Peggy O'Brien, Ed., Teaching Shakespeare Institute
Washington Square Press
New York, 1994

*Shakespeare Set Free: Teaching Twelfth Night and Othello*
Peggy O'Brien, Ed., Teaching Shakespeare Institute
Washington Square Press
New York, 1995

The Shakespeare Set Free series is an invaluable resource with lesson plans, activites, handouts, and excellent suggestions for rehearsing and performing Shakespeare plays in a classroom setting.

*ShakesFear and How to Cure It!*
Ralph Alan Cohen
Prestwick House, Inc.
Delaware, 2006

*The Friendly Shakespeare: A Thoroughly Painless Guide to the Best of the Bard*
Norrie Epstein
Penguin Books
New York, 1994

*Brush Up Your Shakespeare!*
Michael Macrone
Cader Books
New York, 1990

*Shakespeare's Insults: Educating Your Wit*
Wayne F. Hill and Cynthia J. Ottchen
Three Rivers Press
New York, 1991

*Practical Approaches to Teaching Shakespeare*
Peter Reynolds
Oxford University Press
New York, 1991

*Scenes From Shakespeare:*
*A Workbook for Actors*
Robin J. Holt
McFarland and Co.
London, 1988

## THEATER AND PERFORMANCE

*Impro: Improvisation and the Theatre*
Keith Johnstone
Routledge Books
London, 1982

*A Dictionary of Theatre Anthropology:*
*The Secret Art of the Performer*
Eugenio Barba and Nicola Savarese
Routledge
London, 1991

## THEATER GAMES

*Theatre Games for Young Performers*
Maria C. Novelly
Meriwether Publishing
Colorado, 1990

*Improvisation for the Theater*
Viola Spolin
Northwestern University Press
Illinois, 1983

*Theater Games for Rehearsal:*
*A Director's Handbook*
Viola Spolin
Northwestern University Press
Illinois, 1985

*101 Theatre Games for Drama*
*Teachers, Classroom Teachers*
*& Directors*
Mila Johansen
Players Press Inc.
California, 1994

## PLAY DIRECTING

*Theater and the Adolescent Actor:*
*Building a Successful School Program*
Camille L. Poisson
Archon Books
Connecticut, 1994

*Directing for the Theatre*
W. David Sievers
Wm. C. Brown, Co.
Iowa, 1965

*The Director's Vision: Play Direction*
*from Analysis to Production*
Louis E. Catron
Mayfield Publishing Co.
California, 1989

## INTERNET RESOURCES

http://www.folger.edu
The Folger Shakespeare Library's
website has lesson plans, primary
sources, study guides, images,
workshops, programs for teachers
and students, and much more. The
definitive Shakespeare website for
educators, historians and all lovers
of the Bard.

http://www.shakespeare.mit.edu.
The Complete Works of
William Shakespeare.
All complete scripts for *The 30-Minute Shakespeare* series were originally downloaded from this site before editing. Links to other internet resources.

http://www.LoMonico.com/
Shakespeare-and-Media.htm
http://shakespeare-and-media
.wikispaces.com
Michael LoMonico is Senior Consultant on National Education for the Folger Shakespeare Library. His *Seminar Shakespeare 2.0* offers a wealth of information on how to use exciting new approaches and online resources for teaching Shakespeare.

http://www.freesound.org.
A collaborative database of sounds and sound effects.

http://www.wordle.net.
A program for creating "word clouds" from the text that you provide. The clouds give greater prominence to words that appear more frequently in the source text.

http://www.opensourceshakespeare
.org.
This site has good searching capacity.

http://shakespeare.palomar.edu/
default.htm
Excellent links and searches

http://shakespeare.com/
Write like Shakespeare,
Poetry Machine, tag cloud

http://www.shakespeare-online.com/

http://www.bardweb.net/

http://www.rhymezone.com/
shakespeare/
Good searchable word and phrase finder.
Or by lines:
http://www.rhymezone.com/
shakespeare/toplines/

http://shakespeare.mcgill.ca/
Shakespeare and Performance research team

http://www.enotes.com/william-
shakespeare

Needless to say, the internet goes on and on with valuable Shakespeare resources. The ones listed here are excellent starting points and will set you on your way in the great adventure that is Shakespeare.

**NICK NEWLIN** has performed a comedy and variety act for international audiences for twenty-seven years. Since 1996, he has conducted an annual play directing residency affiliated with the Folger Shakespeare Library in Washington, D.C. Newlin received a BA with Honors from Harvard University in 1982 and an MA in Theater with an emphasis in Play Directing from the University of Maryland in 1996.

# THE 30-MINUTE SHAKESPEARE

| | |
|---|---|
| **A MIDSUMMER NIGHT'S DREAM**<br>978-1-935550-00-6 | **ROMEO AND JULIET**<br>978-1-935550-01-3 |
| **MUCH ADO ABOUT NOTHING**<br>978-1-935550-03-7 | **MACBETH**<br>978-1-935550-02-0 |
| **THE MERRY WIVES OF WINDSOR**<br>978-1-935550-05-1 | **TWELFTH NIGHT**<br>978-1-935550-04-4 |

AVAILABLE IN FALL 2010

| | |
|---|---|
| **AS YOU LIKE IT**<br>978-1-935550-06-8 | **LOVE'S LABOR'S LOST**<br>978-1-935550-07-5 |
| **THE COMEDY OF ERRORS**<br>978-1-935550-08-2 | **KING LEAR**<br>978-1-935550-09-9 |
| **HENRY IV, PART 1**<br>978-1-935550-11-2 | **OTHELLO**<br>978-1-935550-10-5 |

All plays $7.95, available in bookstores everywhere

---

*"Nick Newlin's 30-minute play cuttings are perfect for students who have no experience with Shakespeare. Each 30-minute mini-play is a play in itself with a beginning, middle, and end."* —Michael Ellis-Tolaydo, Department of Theater, Film, and Media Studies, St Mary's College of Maryland

**PHOTOCOPYING AND PERFORMANCE RIGHTS**
No part of this publication may be reproduced or transmitted in any form, electronic, photocopying or otherwise, without the prior written permission of the publisher.

There is no royalty for performing *The Merry Wives of Windsor: The 30-Minute Shakespeare* in a classroom or on a stage; however, permission must be obtained for all playscripts used by the actors. The publisher hereby grants unlimited photocopy permission for one series of performances to all acting groups that have purchased at least five (5) copies of the paperback edition or one (1) copy of the downloadable PDF edition available for $12.95 from www.30MinuteShakespeare.com.